WORD PROBLEMS
USING
DECIMALS AND PERCENTAGES

MASTERING MATH WORD PROBLEMS

Zella Williams and
Rebecca Wingard-Nelson

Enslow Publishing
101 W. 23rd Street
Suite 240
New York, NY 10011
USA

enslow.com

Published in 2017 by Enslow Publishing, LLC.
101 W. 23rd Street, Suite 240, New York, NY 10011

Library of Congress Cataloging-in-Publication Data

Names: Williams, Zella, author. | Wingard-Nelson, Rebecca, author.
Title: Word problems using decimals and percentages / Zella Williams and Rebecca Wingard-Nelson.
Description: New York, NY : Enslow Publishing, 2017. | Series: Mastering math word problems | Includes bibliographical references and index.
Identifiers: LCCN 2016032492| ISBN 9780766082588 (library bound) | ISBN 9780766082571 (6 packs) | ISBN 9780766082564 (pbk.)
Subjects: LCSH: Decimal fractions—Juvenile literature. | Percentage—Juvenile literature. | Word problems (Mathematics)—Juvenile literature.
Classification: LCC QA117.W56773 2017 | DDC 513.2/45—dc23
LC record available at https://lccn.loc.gov/2016032492

Printed in China

To Our Readers: We have done our best to make sure all websites in this book were active and appropriate when we went to press. However, the author and the publisher have no control over and assume no liability for the material available on those websites or on any websites they may link to. Any comments or suggestions can be sent by email to customerservice@enslow.com.

Portions of this book originally appeared in the book *Sports Word Problems Starring Decimals and Percents.*

Photo Credits: Cover, p. 1 Kisialiou Yury/Shutterstock.com; pp. 3, 33 Justin Setterfield/Getty Images; p. 4 Blend Images - JGI/Jamie Grill/Getty Images; p. 5 (book) Maximilian Laschon/Shutterstock.com; p. 6 Jamie Grill/Iconica/Getty Images; p. 7 Rich Carey/Shutterstock.com; p. 10 Jacek Chabraszewski/Shutterstock.com; p. 12 Tim Pannell/Corbis/VCG/Getty Images; p. 14 Reuben Schulz/E+/Getty Images; p. 16 Leon Neal/AFP/Getty Images; p. 18 Christian Science Monitor/Getty Images; p. 22 Dejan Milic/Shutterstock.com; p. 24 Michael DeYoung/Blend Images/Getty Images; p.26 Maiava Rusden Sri/Perspectives/Getty Images; p. 27 Airubon/iStock/Thinkstock; p. 29 Beardean/iStock/Thinkstock; p. 31 Flying Colours Ltd/Photodisc/Getty Images; p. 35 Dan Mullan/Getty Images; p. 37 Majority World/Universal Images Group/Getty Images; p. 39 Lilyana Vynogradova/Shutterstock.com; p. 41 Tim Clayton/Corbis Sport/Getty Images; p. 43 Stephen Bonk/Shutterstock.com; p. 47 bluelela/Shutterstock.com; cover and interior pages icons and graphics Shutterstock.com: Anna_leni (owl), Draze Design (pad and pencil), RedlineVector (light bulb), Yuri Gayvoronskiy (eyes), james Weston (scrambled numbers), Ratoca (thumbs up), BeRad (magnifying glass).

Contents

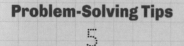

Homework problems are your practice for solving word problems.

Problem-Solving Tips

Word problems come up in lots of places, such as on your homework, on a test, or in your life. Don't let word problems scare you. These tips can help you solve them, no matter where they show up.

Be positive!

Even if it seems hard, you CAN solve word problems. Keep a good attitude. If you make mistakes but keep trying, you should be proud. You learned something new!

Ask for help!

Nobody expects you to be able to solve every problem with no trouble. If you are confused by a problem, ask for help. Soon you'll be solving problems like a pro!

Do your homework!

The more you practice something, the better you become at it. Just like you practice a sport or playing an instrument, you need to practice solving word problems, too. Homework problems are your practice.

In some problems, you will see clue spotters. A magnifying glass will help you spy clue words in the problem.

Move on!

If you get stuck, move to the next problem. Do the ones you know how to solve first. You'll feel more confident. And you won't miss the ones you know because you ran out of time. Go back later and try the problems you skipped.

Take a break!

If you have tried everything you can think of but are only getting frustrated, take a break. Close your eyes and take a deep breath. Stretch your arms and legs. Get a drink of water or a snack. Then come back and try again.

Don't give up!

The first time you try to solve a word problem, you might come up with an answer that does not make sense, or that you know is not right. Don't give up! Try solving the problem a different way. If you quit, you won't learn.

Always check your math after solving a word problem.

Four Easy Steps

Word problems can be solved by following four easy steps.

? **Here's the problem.**

A scuba tank contained 46.3 cubic feet of breathing gas when a diver entered the water. After the dive, 21.3 cubic feet of gas was left. How much gas was used on the dive?

Do you see the yellow scuba tank on this diver's back? The tank holds air so the diver can breathe while under water.

  Step 1 Read and understand the problem.

Read the problem carefully.

Ask yourself questions, like:

What do you know?

You know the amount of gas in the tank before the dive (46.3 cubic feet) and after the dive (21.3 cubic feet).

What are you trying to find?

How much gas was used on the dive.

What is happening in the problem?

The tank starts with some gas, then some is used.

Are there any clue words?

Yes, the word "left" tells you this is a subtraction problem.

Step 2 Make a plan.

Some problems tell you how they should be solved. They may say "**draw a picture**," or "**write an equation.**" For other problems, you will need to make your own plan. Most problems can be solved in more than one way. Some plans you might try are:

Look for a pattern	**Write an equation**
Draw a picture	**Use a model**
Estimate	**Break it apart**

How can you solve this problem?

You can write a subtraction equation.

Step 3 Solve the problem.

It is time to do the math!

If you find that your plan is not working, make a new plan. Don't give up the first time. Write your answer. Make sure you include the units.

Let's write the equation.

Start with the amount of gas before the dive. Subtract the amount of gas that was left after the dive to find how much was used.

```
   46.3 cubic feet
 − 21.3 cubic feet
   25.0 cubic feet
```

When you add or subtract decimal numbers, line up the decimal points, then add or subtract just like a whole number.

25.0 cubic feet of breathing gas was used on the dive.

Step 4 Look back.

The problem is solved! But you aren't finished yet. Take a good look at your answer.

Does it make sense? Did you include the units? Did you use the right numbers to begin?

Estimate or use the inverse operation to check your math.

Is there another plan you could have used to solve the problem?

One way to check the math is to use the opposite, or inverse, operation. Addition and subtraction are opposites, so use addition to check this problem.

Add the answer (25.0) and
the number you subtracted (21.3)

```
  25.0
+ 21.3
  46.3
```

If the sum (46.3) is the number you started with, then your answer is correct.

Did you start with 46.3? Yes.

Tools to Help You Solve Problems

Clue Words

Sometimes a word problem has clue words in it. These words are tools that can help you figure out how to solve the problem.

Here's the problem.

Cory ran 2.1 miles in the morning and 3.7 miles in the afternoon. How many total miles did he run?

People run to stay fit and healthy.

Problems that combine values, like miles, are addition problems.

In this problem, the clue word "total" tells you to add the morning distance and the afternoon distance.

Some other clue words that tell you a problem might use addition are: **add**, **and**, **combined**, **sum**, **plus**, **more**, **together**, **increase**, and **both**.

? Here's another problem.

Cory ran 2.1 miles in the morning and 3.7 miles in the afternoon. How much farther did he run in the afternoon than he did in the morning?

Problems that find the difference between two values, like miles, are subtraction problems. Problems that start with a value then take some away also use subtraction.

In this problem, the clue words "how much farther" tell you to find the difference between the morning and afternoon distances. Some other clue words that tell you a problem might use subtraction are: **subtract**, **difference**, **take away**, **how much less**, **how many more**, **remain**, **left**, **fewer**, and **compare**.

? Here's another problem that uses clue words to help you figure out which operation is needed.

Kate drank 1.5 quarts of water per game at each of her soccer games. She had two games. How much water did she drink?

It is important to drink lots of water when you are being physically active.

Problems that combine quantities of the same size are multiplication problems.

In this problem, the clue word "per" tells you to combine two quantities of 1.5 quarts. This is a multiplication problem. Some other clue words that tell you a problem might use multiplication are: **at**, **every**, **multiply**, **of**, **product**, **rate**, **times**, and **twice**.

Say you knew Kate had three quarts of water and played two games. How many quarts did she have on average for each game.

Problems that take a value and separate it into equal parts are division problems.

In this problem, the clue word "**average**" tells you to separate the total amount of water into the amount of water per game. This is division. Some other clue words that tell you a problem might use division are: **divided**, **each**, **equally**, **evenly**, **every**, **half**, **per**, and **split**.

! Opposite Problems

Let's look at the water problem. Using the same facts, we wrote two problems.

Here are the facts:

Kate drank 3 quarts of water

She drank 1.5 quarts of water at each game.

She played 2 games.

Multiplication:

1.5 quarts per game $\times$ 2 games = 3 quarts

Division:

3 quarts $\div$ 2 games = 1.5 quarts per game

Because they are related, operations that are the opposites sometimes use the same clue words, like "per" and "each." The clue words will help you get started, but you must understand what is happening in the problem.

! Draw a Picture

Pictures are problem-solving tools, too. They can help you understand and solve problems.

? Here's the problem.

In the sport of curling, a stone is pushed over the ice toward a target. The closest stone to the center scores a point. One stone stopped

0.8 meters from the center of the target. Another stopped 0.6 meters from the center. Which stone would score a point?

In curling, there are sweepers who help the stone move faster or slower toward the target.

Read and understand.

What do you know?

Two stones were thrown. One stopped 0.8 meters from the center. The other stopped 0.6 meters from the center.

What are you trying to find?

Which stone would score a point. The closer stone scores, so the question is which stone is closer to the center of the target.

What is happening in the problem?

This problem asks which stone is closer to the center, so it is comparing two distances. You are trying to find the smaller distance.

Plan.

Let's draw a picture.

Solve.

Draw a picture of a target. Then show in the picture how far each stone stopped from the target. This picture is drawn to show each tenth of a meter from the target. The first stone is drawn in red and the second in blue.

The second stone, at 0.6 meters, is closer to the target, so it would score a point.

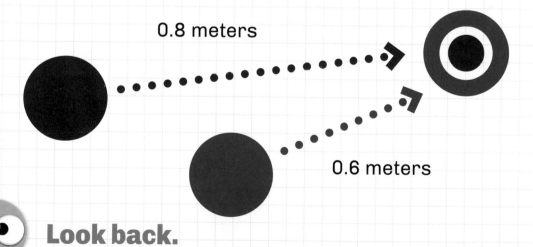

0.8 meters

0.6 meters

Look back.

Could you have solved this problem another way? Yes, you can compare 0.6 and 0.8. Since 0.6 < 0.8, the stone at 0.6 meters is closer, so it scores a point.

Use a Model

There are many kinds of models. You can use items, like beans, cubes, or sticks, to model a problem. Or you can use models on paper, like number lines, diagrams, or graphs.

Here's the problem.

An Olympic luge course is exactly 1,341.2 meters long. To the nearest meter, how long is the course?

Lugers lie on their backs and slide feet first down an icy chute at up to 90 miles per hour.

Read and understand.

What do you know?
The course is 1,341.2 m long.

What are you trying to find?

The length of the course to the nearest meter.

Plan.

Let's use a number line model.

Solve.

Draw a number line to show tenths from the whole number 1,341 to the whole number 1,342.

1,341.0 1,341.1 1,341.2 1,341.3 1,341.4 1,341.5 1,341.6 1,341.7 1,341.8 1,341.9 1,342.0

Mark 1,341.2 on the number line. Is 1,341.2 closer to 1,341 or to 1,342?

To the nearest whole meter, the course is 1,341 meters long.

Look back.

Could you have solved this problem another way?

Yes, you can round the decimal 1,341.2 to the nearest whole number. Since a 2 is in the tenths place, 1,341.2 rounds down to 1,341. The answer is the same either way.

Equations

Some word problems can be changed easily into equations. Equations are number sentences that use an equal sign.

Here's the problem.

Ziva bought two rock-climbing ropes. The shorter one cost $47.50 and the longer one cost $92.25. How much did the ropes cost together?

Rock climbers wear a special harness and are tied to ropes to keep them safe if they fall.

Read and understand.

What do you know?
Ziva bought two ropes. One rope cost $47.50 and the other cost $92.25.

What are you trying to find?
The cost of the two ropes together.

Are there any clue words in the problem?
Yes. The clue word "together" tells you this is an addition problem.

Plan.

Let's write an addition equation.

Solve.

One way to write an equation is to write a sentence that shows what happens in the problem first. Use the word "equals" or "is."

The cost of one rope plus the cost of the other rope equals the cost of the ropes together.

Change the words in the sentence to the numbers you know from the problem. Use symbols for words like plus (+) and equals (=).

$$\$47.50 + \$92.25 = \text{the cost of the ropes together.}$$

Now do the math. Remember to line up the decimal points.

$$\begin{array}{r} \$47.50 \\ + \$92.25 \\ \hline \$139.75 \end{array}$$

Together, the ropes cost $139.75.

Look back.

Does the answer make sense?

Yes.

Why? When you estimate using whole dollars, you find $48 + $92 = $140. The answer is close to the estimate.

Use a Table

Sometimes you need to find information in a table before you can solve a problem.

Here's the problem.

The average shoe size for a man is size 10. A professional basketball player's shoe size is closer to size 20. Use information from the table below to find the **difference** in length (centimeters, cm) between a size 10 and a size 20 shoe.

Shoe Size	Heel-to-Toe Length (cm)
10	27.8
12	28.73
14	30.48
16	32.23
18	33.81
20	35.56

 Read and understand.

What do you know?

An average man's shoe size is 10. A professional basketball player's shoe size is 20.

What are you trying to find?

The difference in length (in centimeters, cm) between a size 10 and a size 20 shoe.

What kind of problem is this?

This is a subtraction problem. It uses the clue word "difference."

Plan.

The problem doesn't give all of the information. Get the information from the table, then subtract.

Solve.

From the table, find the length of a size 10 shoe (27.8 cm) and a size 20 shoe (35.56 cm).

Subtract. Remember to line up the decimal points.

$$
\begin{array}{r}
35.56 \\
-\,27.80 \\
\hline
7.76
\end{array}
$$

A size 20 shoe is 7.76 cm longer than a size 10.

Look back.

Is the subtraction correct?

Let's check by doing the inverse operation. $7.76 + 27.80 = 35.56$

Yes! It is correct.

Find the Hidden Information

Some problems use words like twice (times 2) and dozen (12) to give you information without numbers. Other problems ask you to use information you already know.

? Here's the problem.

Eva is training to run a marathon. Each day she runs 5.2 kilometers. How many kilometers does she run in a week?

It takes a lot of work to get ready for a marathon. It is important to eat healthy foods and drink plenty of water, too.

Read and understand.

What does the problem tell you?

Eva runs 5.2 kilometers each day.

What are you trying to find?

The number of kilometers Eva runs in a week.

Is there any hidden information? Yes. To solve this problem, you must know that a "week" means seven days.

What kind of problem is this?

The clue word "each" tells you this could be a multiplication problem. You are combining the same value (5.2 km) a number of times (7), so this is a multiplication problem.

Plan.

Let's write an equation.

Solve.

Write a multiplication equation that uses the numbers you know.

5.2 kilometers × 7 days = total kilometers in a week

$$\begin{array}{r} 5.2 \\ \times\ 7 \\ \hline 36.4 \end{array}$$

Multiply decimal numbers just like whole numbers, then put in the decimal point.

5.2 × 7 = 36.4

Eva runs 36.4 kilometers in a week.

Look back.

Is the answer reasonable?

Yes.

Why? Estimate the answer by rounding the decimal 5.2 to a whole number 5, then multiplying.

5 × 7 = 35.

The answer (36.4) is a little greater than the estimate (35), so it makes sense.

More Ways to Solve Problems

! Patterns in Tens

When a number is multiplied by a power of ten, such as 10, 100, or 1,000, you can multiply by moving the decimal point. Pretty easy, right?

? Here's the problem.

Ian wants to snowboard down a slope at least 10 times today. In 16.2 minutes, he can ride the lift to the top of the slope and then snowboard down. At this rate, how many minutes will it take Ian to ride the slope 10 times?

Snowboarding became an official Olympic event in Nagano, Japan, in 1998.

Read and understand.

What do you know?

Ian wants to snowboard down a slope at least 10 times. It takes 16.2 minutes to ride up the lift and then snowboard down the slope.

What are you trying to find?

How many minutes it will take to snowboard the slope 10 times.

Plan.

Let's use mental math.

Solve.

When you multiply a number by a power of 10, the decimal point moves one place value to the right for each zero. It moves one place for 10, two places for 100, and so on.

$16.2 \times 10 = 162$

It will take Ian 162 minutes to snowboard the slope 10 times.

Look back.

Did you answer the right question?
Yes.

Does your answer make sense?
Yes.

You can use what you know about tens for other problems like this one.

How many minutes would it take Ian to snowboard this slope 100 times?

$16.2 \times 100 = 1,620$ minutes.

! Division Equations

Problems that take a value and divide it into smaller equal values are division problems.

? Here's the problem.

While playing 18 holes of golf, Esther and Sam walked 3.6 miles. If they walked an equal distance for each hole, how far did they walk per hole?

Golfers typically play 9 or 18 holes. They want to get their ball in the hole with the fewest strokes.

Read and understand.

What do you know?

Esther and Sam walked 3.6 miles.
They played 18 holes of golf.

What are you trying to find?

How far they walked per hole.

There are 336 dimples on a regulation golf ball.

Are there any clue words in the problem?

Yes, the word "per" tells you this could be multiplication or division. You start with the full distance walked, and you want to find smaller equal distances. This is a division problem.

Plan.

Let's write an equation.

Solve.

Use the numbers you know to write an equation.

3.6 miles ÷ 18 holes = miles per hole

Use the long division symbol to divide decimals just like whole numbers. Put a decimal point in the answer above the decimal point in the dividend.

Divide.

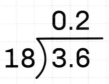

Esther and Sam walked 0.2 miles per hole.

Look back.

Did you start with the right numbers?

Yes.

Is the math correct?

Use multiplication to check division. Multiply the answer, 0.2, by the number you divided by, 18.

$0.2 \times 18 = 3.6$ The math is correct.

Estimate

When you don't need an exact answer, you can estimate.

Here's the problem.

Lauren is on the lacrosse team. She is buying a uniform for $70.35, a practice stick for $29.50, and new cleats for $79.89. About how much money does she need all together?

Lacrosse was originally played by Native Americans and introduced to Europeans who came to settle in North America. The game is much different from the original, but it is still lots of fun.

Read and understand.

What do you know?
Lauren is buying:
a uniform for $70.35
a practice stick for $29.50
new cleats for $79.89

What are you trying to find?
About how much money she needs all together.

Are there any clue words?
Yes. The words "all together" tell you this is an addition problem.

Plan.

The problem does not ask for an exact answer, so let's estimate.

Solve.

You can estimate the answer to an addition problem by rounding each decimal to the nearest whole number, then adding.

$70.35 rounds to $70.00.

$29.50 rounds to $30.00

$79.89 rounds to $80.00.

$70.00
$30.00
+ $80.00
_____
$180.00

Lauren needs about $180.00 all together.

Look back.

Does the answer make sense?

Yes.

Did you include the units in the answer?

Yes.

Decimal Statistics

Statistics in sports are often given in decimals. Knowing how the decimal was figured helps you understand what it means.

?   ## Here's the problem.

Batting averages are three-digit decimals found by dividing the number of times a player got a hit by the number of times the player was at bat. Alonzo was at bat eight times. If he got six hits, what is his batting average?

There are more than 2.1 million players in Little League Baseball world wide.

Read and understand.

What do you know?
Alonzo was at bat eight times. He had six hits.

What are you trying to find?

Alonzo's batting average.

Plan.

The problem tells you the batting average is the number of hits divided by the number of at-bats. Write a division equation.

Solve.

Use the numbers you know to write an equation.

6 hits ÷ 8 at-bats = Alonzo's batting average.

Divide. Use a long division symbol. Remember, the number that is first in the equation is the one that goes inside the symbol.

$$8 \overline{)6} = 0.75$$

$6 \div 8 = 0.75$

Alonzo's batting average is 0.75.

Look back.

Did you answer the right question?

Yes.

Read the question again. Did you miss any information?

Yes. A batting average is a three-digit number. To write 0.75 as a three-digit decimal, add a zero on the right. Alonzo's batting average is 0.750.

Problems with Percents

We are going to do a few problems that use percents. A percent is a decimal that shows parts of 100. For example, 50 out of 100 is 50% or .50.

! ## More Than One Question

Some problems ask you more than one question. When there is more than one question, you should have more than one answer.

? ### Here's the problem.

An ice sledge hockey team is getting ready for the Paralympics. They have won 72 of their 100 games. What percent of the games have they won? What percent have they not won?

Two players fight for the puck in this sledge hockey game between Russia and Norway during the Paralympic Winter Games.

Read and understand.

What do you know?

The team played 100 games.

They won 72 of the games.

What are you trying to find?

The percent of games won and the percent of games not won.

Plan.

There are two questions.

The first asks for the percent of games won. Write the number of wins as a percent.

The second question asks for the percent of games not won. Use subtraction to find how many games were not won, then write it as a percent.

Solve.

Write 72 games won out of 100 as a percent. When a value is out of 100, you can write it as a percent just by adding the percent sign.

72 out of 100 = 72%

72% of the games were won.

Total games	–	Games won	=	Games not won
100	–	72	=	28 not won

Write 28 games not won out of 100 as a percent.

28 out of 100 = 28%

28% of the games were lost.

Look back.

Is the math correct? The number of games won plus the number of games not won should equal all of the games.

72 won + 28 not won = 100 games played

Decimals as Percents

To write a decimal as a percent, multiply the decimal by 100.

Here's the problem.

In football, a completion statistic is a decimal or percent that tells how many passes were caught by a receiver. If a quarterback has a completion statistic of 0.526, what percent of his passes were completed?

Football is a fun sport. The goal is to get touchdowns and field goals, while stopping the other team from doing the same.

Read and understand.

What do you know?

The quarterback has a 0.526 completion statistic.

What are you trying to find?

The percent of passes that were completed.

Are there any clue words?

No. This problem asks you to change a decimal to a percent, not perform an operation.

Plan.

The completion statistic is given as a decimal. The problem asks for a percent.

Let's change the decimal to a percent.

Solve.

A percent tells you how many out of 100. To change a decimal to a percent, multiply it by 100.

0.526 × 100 = percent of completions

0.526 × 100 = 52.6

Move the decimal point two place values to the right.

0.526 = 52.6%

52.6% of the passes were completed.

Look back.

Did you start with the right numbers?

Yes.

! Percents as Decimals

Write a percent as a decimal by dividing the percent by 100.

? Here's the problem.

In taekwondo, when a competitor has a 7-point lead in a sparring match, he wins immediately and the match ends. John has won 63% of his matches this way. Write 63% as a decimal.

Taekwondo is a Korean martial art that focuses on fast kicking techniques.

Read and understand.

What do you know?
John has won 63% of his matches by having a 7-point lead.

What are you trying to find?
The decimal that is equal to 63%.

Plan.

Let's change the percent to a decimal.

Solve.

To change a percent to a decimal, divide by 100.

$63 \div 100 = 0.63$

When you divide a number by 100, move the decimal point two place values to the left.

$63\% = 0.63$

Look back.

Did you remember to include the units in your answer?

The question does not have any units.

Did you move the decimal point the right number of places?

Yes, dividing by 100 moves the decimal point two places to the left.

Percents and Division

To find what percent one number is of another, use division.

Here's the problem.

There are 50 students in Emily's gymnastics class. Twelve of them are working on the uneven bars. What percent of the students are working on the uneven bars?

Uneven bars are one of four events in women's artistic gymnastics. The others are floor, vault, and beam.

Read and understand.

What do you know?

There are 50 students in the class.

Twelve students are working on the uneven bars.

What are you trying to find?

The percent of students who are working on the uneven bars.

What kind of problem is this?

The problem asks what percent 12 is of 50.

It is a division problem.

Plan.

Write an equation that divides the part by the whole.

Solve.

The whole is 50 students in the class.

The part is 12 students working on the uneven bars.

$12 \div 50 = 0.24$

The answer to the division problem is a decimal, but the question asks for a percent.

Change the decimal to a percent.

$0.24 = 24\%$

24% of the students are working on the uneven bars.

Look back.

Does your answer make sense?

Yes. When you double 12 out of 50, you get 24 out of 100. Twenty-four out of 100 is 24%.

The Percent Equation

The percent equation shows how three numbers—a percent, a whole, and a part—are related.

Here's the problem.

Stefan has won 50% of his wrestling matches. He has competed in 16 matches. How many has he won?

Read and understand.

What do you know?

Stefan has competed in 16 wrestling matches. He has won 50% of his matches.

What are you trying to find?

How many matches Stefan has won.

Are there any clue words?

Yes, the clue word "of" tells you this might be a multiplication problem.

Plan.

Write a multiplication equation.

Wrestling has been a sport for thousands of years. Today most people practice Greco-Roman wrestling.

Solve.

The percent equation uses multiplication to relate a whole, a percent, and a part.

The percent equation says:

A percent of a whole is a part.

In math, this means percent × whole = part.

Put the numbers you know in the percent equation. You know the whole, or the total number of matches, is 16. You know the percent is 50%.

50%	×	16	=	Number of matches won
(percent)		(whole)		(part)

Change 50% to the decimal 0.50, or 0.5.

0.5 × 16 = number of matches won.

Multiply. 0.50 × 16 = 8.0

Stefan has won eight wrestling matches.

Look back.

Is the answer reasonable? Yes. 50% means 50 of 100. 50 is half of 100. Eight is half of 16.

Break It Apart

To solve some problems, you need more than one operation.

Here's the problem.

A shop that rents surfboards will take 20% off the rental price of $20.00 per hour if a group rents together. What is the price of a board per hour if you are in a group?

Read and understand.

What do you know?

The regular rental price is $20.00 per hour. For a group, the price is 20% less.

What are you trying to find?

The price per hour if you are in a group.

Surfing is a sport in which a person stands on a board in the ocean and rides waves in to the shore.

Plan.

To solve this problem, you need to find the amount that is taken off, then subtract to find the new price.

Let's break it into parts.

Solve.

You know the regular price. You know the percent. Use the percent equation to find the amount that is taken off if you are in a group.

Percent × whole = part

20%	×	$20.00	=	amount taken off
0.2	×	$20.00	=	$4.00 off

Subtract the amount taken off from the regular price to find the price if you are in a group.

$20.00 − $4.00 = $16.00

If you are in a group, the rental price per board is $16.00 per hour.

Look back.

Does your answer make sense?

Yes.

Is there another way to solve this problem?

Yes. If you get 20% off, then you pay 80%. You can find 80% of $20.00, which is $16.00.

Remember the Plan

To solve a word problem, follow these steps:

Read and understand the problem.

Know what the problem says and what you need to find.

If you don't understand, ask questions before you start.

Make a plan.

Choose the plan that makes the most sense and is easiest for you. Remember, there is usually more than one way to find the right answer.

Solve the problem.

Use the plan. If your first plan isn't working, try a different one. Take a break and come back with a fresh mind.

Look back.

Read the problem again. Make sure your answer makes sense. Check your math. If the answer does not look right, don't give up now! Use what you've learned to go back and try the problem again.

Glossary

addition One of the four basic operations in math; the process of adding two or more numbers together.

compare To look at two different equations or situations to show different levels of quality, quantity, or relation.

decimal A number that indicates a part of a whole by using a decimal point.

division One of the four basic operations in math; the process of finding out how many times a smaller number is contained within a larger one.

equations Number sentences that have two expressions that are equal in value on either side of the equals sign.

estimation A rough calculation of the number, quantity, or value of something.

multiplication One of the four basic operations in math; the process of repeated addition.

operation A math process, such as addition, subtraction, multiplication, or division.

percent A number that shows part of 100 that is converted from a decimal.

subtraction One of the four basic operations in math; the process of taking a number away from a larger number.

unit Whatever object that is being added or subtracted, such as spines or stripes.

For More Information

Books

Adler, David. *Fractions, Decimals, and Percents.* New York, NY: Holiday House, 2010.

Greenberg, Dan. *Fractured Math Fairy Tales: Fractions & Decimals.* New York, NY: Scholastic, 2005.

Lee, Cora. *The Great Number Rumble: A Story of Math in Surprising Places.* Buffalo, NY: Firefly Books, Inc., 2007.

Websites

Aplusmath
www.aplusmath.com
Interactive math resources for teachers, parents, and students featuring free math worksheets, math games, math flashcards, and more.

Coolmath Games
www.coolmath-games.com
Try your hand at games that make learning and practicing math fun.

Math Playground
www.mathplayground.com/wordproblems.html
Solve math word problems with Thinking Blocks, Jake and Astro, and more.

Index